THE REAL WORLD

D0548610

The Indian Subcontinent

Anita Ganeri

01741

Watts Books
London • New York • Sydney

© 1994 Watts Books

Watts Books
96 Leonard Street
London EC2A 4RH

Franklin Watts Australia
14 Mars Road
Lane Cove
NSW 2066

UK ISBN: 0 7496 1221 5

10 9 8 7 6 5 4 3 2 1

Dewey Decimal Classification 915.4

A CIP catalogue record for this book
is available from the British Library

Series consultant: Anna Sandeman
Editor: Jane Walker
Design: Ron Kamen, Green Door Design Ltd
Cover design: Mike Davis
Maps: Mainline Design
        Visual Image
Additional artwork: Mainline Design
                    Visual Image
Cover artwork: Raymond Turvey
Fact checking: Simone K. Lefolii
Research: Jonardon Ganeri
Picture research: Alison Renwick

Cover photographs: left, Supreme Courts, Lahore, Pakistan (Christine Osborne Pictures);
centre, Street dwellers in Delhi, India (Christine Osborne Pictures); right, Karakoram
Highway, Pakistan (Christine Osborne Pictures).

Photographic credits: (t = top, m = middle, b = bottom): Associated Press 13(t); J. Allan
Cash 11(m), 16(b); Colorific! 5(m) Penny Tweedie; Chris Fairclough Colour Library 7(b),
8(b), 25(b); Robert Harding Picture Library 14, 17(m) G. Hellier, 22(b) David Lomax,
23(m), 25(m) Duncan Maxwell; Jim Holmes 5(t) Royal Geographical Society, 6, 7(t),
13(b), 15(b), 16(t), 18, 19(b), 21(m), 22(t); Hutchison Library 17(b) N. Durrell McKenna,
25(t), 26(b) Christine Pemberton, 27 Liba Taylor, 29; Christine Osborne Pictures 7(m),
8(t), 10, 11(t), 15(t), 19(m), 21(t), (b), 23(b), 26(t); Frank Spooner Pictures 5(b)
Bartholomew/Liaison, 9 Bartholomew/Liaison, 32 Bartholomew/Liaison.

Artwork credit: The village plan on p.17 is based on a plan originally reproduced
in *India: Paths to Development*, published by Oxfam.

Printed in Belgium

Contents

Where is the subcontinent?

The Indian subcontinent covers some four million square kilometres of the southern part of Asia, the world's largest continent. The area is often referred to as South Asia. It includes the countries of India, Pakistan, Bangladesh, Sri Lanka, Nepal and Bhutan. It is fringed by the Indian Ocean, the Arabian Sea and the Bay of Bengal. The subcontinent is a vast area, where at least one-fifth of the world's people live. This huge and rapidly growing population is one of the subcontinent's most serious problems. The land and natural resources will simply not be able to support too many more people.

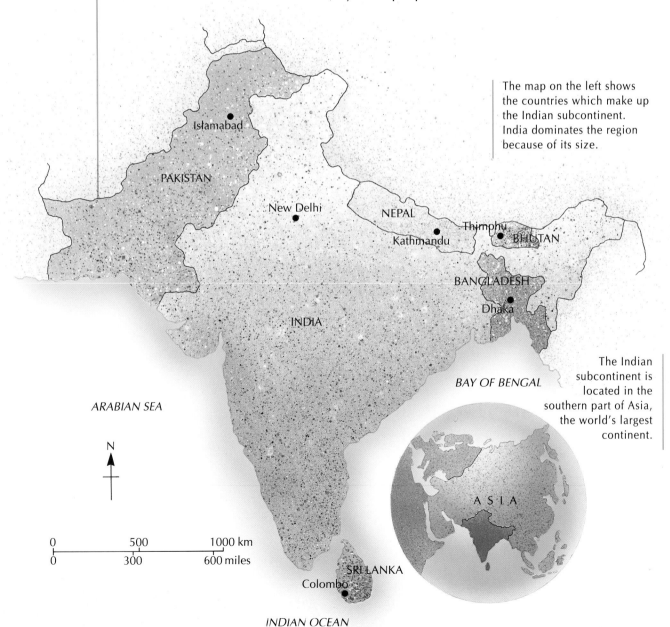

The map on the left shows the countries which make up the Indian subcontinent. India dominates the region because of its size.

The Indian subcontinent is located in the southern part of Asia, the world's largest continent.

Islamabad

PAKISTAN

New Delhi

NEPAL

Thimphu

Kathmandu

BHUTAN

BANGLADESH

Dhaka

INDIA

BAY OF BENGAL

ARABIAN SEA

N

0   500   1000 km
0   300   600 miles

ASIA

SRI LANKA

Colombo

INDIAN OCEAN

After independence

With the exception of Nepal and Bhutan, most of the subcontinent formed part of the British Empire in the nineteenth and early twentieth centuries. India and Sri Lanka regained their independence in the 1940s, when the new country of Pakistan was also created. Bangladesh came into being in 1971.

Since gaining their independence, all these countries have tried to develop their economies and societies. The people of the subcontinent are mostly poor by Western standards. Efforts are being made to improve their standard of living. Improvements in agriculture and industry have been particularly successful.

The Taj Mahal in India was built in the seventeenth century by the Mughal emperor, Shah Jahan, as a memorial for his wife. It is one of the subcontinent's most visited landmarks.

Heavy flooding is a regular problem in the low-lying coastal areas of Bangladesh (left). In 1992, Pakistan's worst floods for decades left at least 2,000 people dead and around 3 million homeless.

Regional images

For 4,500 years, the Indian subcontinent has been a major centre of civilisation. It has been invaded many times, mainly along its north-west borders. As a result, today it is a melting pot of different images and influences. Among the people of the subcontinent, there are many different cultures, beliefs and languages.

The geography of the subcontinent also affects the images of the region which we see in the news. For example, in 1992, serious flooding occurred in Pakistan and Bangladesh after local rivers had burst their banks.

Religion is another driving force behind life and current events in the subcontinent. Long-standing rivalry between Hindu and Muslim groups in India, for example, continues to make the headlines. In the early 1990s, religious violence broke out in the town of Ayodhya (below) in India. Fanatical Hindus destroyed a Muslim mosque.

A vast landscape

The Indian subcontinent is, in fact, a separate physical region. The hard crust around the Earth is divided into a number of huge sections, called plates. Over millions of years, these plates have drifted on top of the layer of liquid rock beneath them. In this way the size and position of the Earth's continents have changed.

The Indian subcontinent is part of the Indo-Australian plate and was once attached to Australia. It moved northwards and crashed into the Eurasian plate about 40 million years ago. The sea-bed between the two plates was pushed upwards by this massive collision, forming a great range of mountains, the Himalayas. These mark the northern boundary between the subcontinent and the rest of Asia. The two tiny kingdoms of Nepal and Bhutan lie among the Himalayas.

The map shows the physical geography of the Indian subcontinent – its major mountain ranges, rivers, plains and so on.

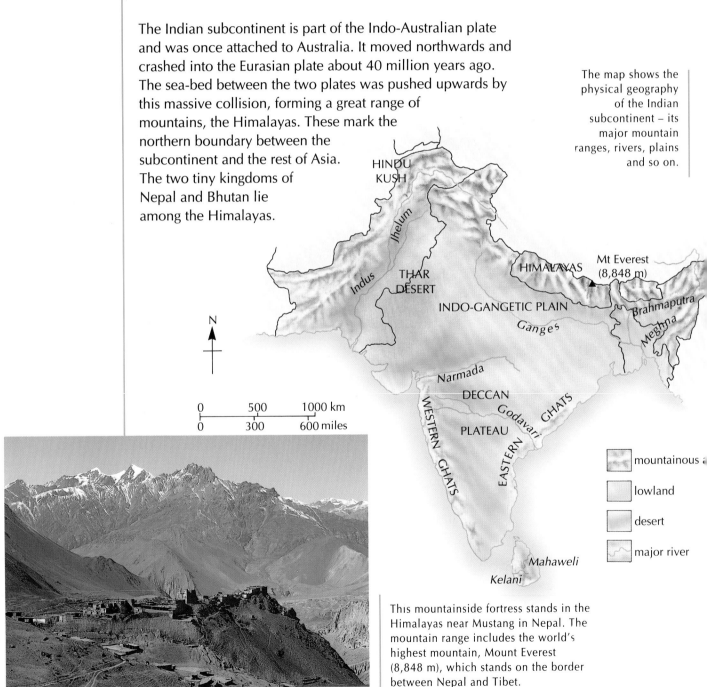

HINDU KUSH

Jhelum

Indus

THAR DESERT

HIMALAYAS

Mt Everest (8,848 m)

INDO-GANGETIC PLAIN

Ganges

Brahmaputra

Meghna

Narmada

DECCAN

Godavari

PLATEAU

WESTERN GHATS

EASTERN GHATS

Mahaweli

Kelani

N

| 0 | 500 | 1000 km |
| 0 | 300 | 600 miles |

mountainous

lowland

desert

major river

This mountainside fortress stands in the Himalayas near Mustang in Nepal. The mountain range includes the world's highest mountain, Mount Everest (8,848 m), which stands on the border between Nepal and Tibet.

A varied geography

The vast subcontinent has a very varied landscape, ranging from snow-capped mountains to tropical rainforest, to sandy desert. There are four major geographical areas. In the north lie the Himalayas and related mountains. The Himalayas are the world's highest mountains, with more than 80 peaks over 7,500 metres high. To the south is the triangular-shaped part of India, known as peninsular India. In the west, the Thar Desert covers an area of more than 200,000 square kilometres. Lastly, the Indo-Gangetic Plain stretches from the River Indus in Pakistan right across India to the Ganges Delta in Bangladesh. Here the river flows into the Bay of Bengal. Ninety per cent of Bangladesh's surface is taken up by the delta area of the Ganges and Brahmaputra rivers.

View across the Thar Desert from Kot Diji in Pakistan. The desert reaches from the western Indian state of Rajasthan across the border into eastern Pakistan.

The south coast of Sri Lanka is lined with sandy beaches, fringed with tropical palm trees.

Life along the rivers

The first great civilisation in the subcontinent flourished along the banks of the River Indus, in modern-day Pakistan, in 2500 BC. It was known as the Indus Valley Civilisation.

Rivers play an important role in the subcontinent today. The Indo-Gangetic Plain is one of the most densely populated regions in the world. Its fertile soils support about half the population of the subcontinent. As the River Ganges flows out into the Bay of Bengal, it deposits small islands of silt in the delta. These islands are very fertile and attract many farmers, despite the terrible risk of flooding and cyclones in this area (see page 9).

The River Indus was the life-blood of the ancient civilisation which grew up in its valley. Farmers grew crops in the rich silty soil which was deposited when the river flooded. The downfall of the Indus people in about 2000 BC may have been caused by a combination of serious floods and changes in the river's course, which left the valuable farmland dry and infertile.

Monsoons and seasons

The Indian subcontinent has a wide range of climates. In India, for example, rainfall varies considerably. While parts of the western desert receive less than 6.5 centimetres of rain a year, in the north-east 20 metres of rain may fall each year. Average temperatures range from about 10°C to 40°C. Bangladesh has a tropical monsoon climate, while the climate of Pakistan is generally hot and dry. In the far south of the subcontinent, Sri Lanka has a tropical climate. In the far north, the climate in Nepal and Bhutan becomes colder as you reach higher up the mountains.

It is unbearably hot in parts of India during the hot season. Some of the highest temperatures are recorded on the northern plains. Thunderstorms herald the beginning of the wet season.

The mighty monsoon

The Indian climate is dominated by monsoon winds. The term 'monsoon' refers to winds which change direction according to the time of year. The monsoon blows from the south-west in summer, changes direction, and then blows from the north-east in winter. The south-west monsoon is the most important of the two. It arrives in India in June, bringing torrential rain. India's farmers rely on the monsoon rains to water their crops and ensure a good harvest. The south-west monsoon brings with it about two-thirds of the country's annual rainfall. In a largely agricultural society like India, the failure of the monsoon spells disaster.

In northern India the monsoon divides the year into three seasons – wet, cool and hot. The rains finish in September, bringing the wet season to a close. The cool season lasts from October to March. January is the coolest month of the year, with temperatures dropping to about 10°C. In March, the hot season begins and the temperature rises quickly. May is the hottest month. Temperatures can rise to over 45°C in some areas. In southern India temperatures are hot all year round.

Temperatures in the mountains begin to fall the higher up you go. On the mountain tops, it is always so cold that the ice never melts.

8

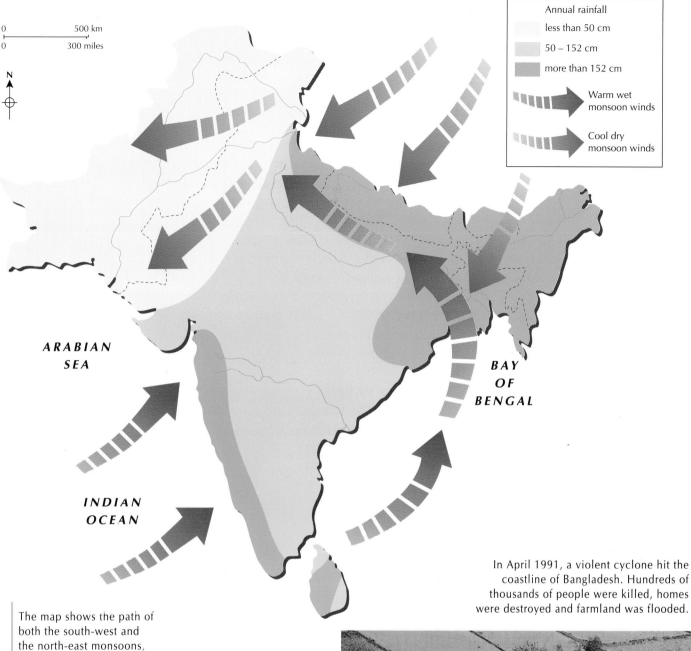

ARABIAN
SEA

BAY
OF
BENGAL

INDIAN
OCEAN

The map shows the path of both the south-west and the north-east monsoons, as well as the annual rainfall across the subcontinent

In April 1991, a violent cyclone hit the coastline of Bangladesh. Hundreds of thousands of people were killed, homes were destroyed and farmland was flooded.

Weather extremes

Too much or too little rain means loss of food and income for the subcontinent's farmers. Flooding is common in the delta region of Bangladesh. This area also suffers devastating tropical storms, called cyclones, at the end of the wet season. If the rivers do not flood, no fertile silt is deposited in which the farmers can grow their crops. Yet if the floods are too heavy, any crops are quickly washed away.

Peoples and population

The Indian subcontinent is one of the most densely populated areas on Earth. After China, India is the world's second most populous country, with about 850 million people, or around one in five of all the people in the world. The population of the whole subcontinent is about 1,130 million. This number is set to rise by about two per cent a year. India's population is likely to reach one billion by the year 2000. At present, over 25 million babies are born each year in India. Family planning is now an essential part of the subcontinent's future.

Children in a Punjabi village, Pakistan.

Life expectancy

One of the reasons for large families on the subcontinent is the high death rate among babies and young children. About one in ten babies die before their first birthday. People also have large families because parents rely on their children to share their workload and to look after them in old age. Life expectancy for adults is about 59 years in India but only 46 years in Bhutan.

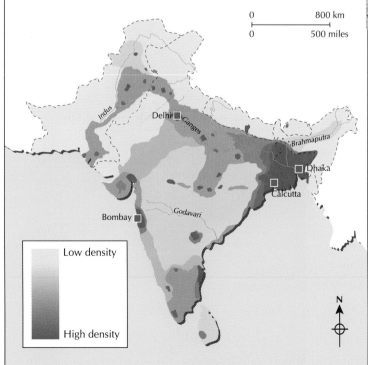

0   800 km

0   500 miles

Low density

High density

The map shows the distribution of the population of the Indian subcontinent. People are not evenly spread throughout the region. More people live along the Ganges, Indus and Brahmaputra rivers, and along the coasts, than anywhere else.

This tribal woman comes from Goa in western India. The traditional way of life of many *adivasis* is under threat from the exploitation of the natural resources found in their forest homes.

People and origins

The people of the subcontinent tend to look physically different, depending on which region they come from. People from the south and east are usually shorter and darker skinned than people in the north. Regional differences can also be seen in the types of food that people eat and in the clothes they wear.

In India, there are about 400 tribal groups. Most live in central and eastern India. They are known as *adivasis*, which means 'original people'. They have lived in the forests, hunting and gathering food, for thousands of years. Today, however, their forest homes are being cleared to provide timber or to gain access to mineral resources. Some forest areas have been flooded during the building of large dams.

A wealth of languages

A wide range of languages is spoken across the subcontinent. Hindi is the national language of India, although it is mainly spoken in the north of the country. India also has 14 other official languages, 13 of which correspond to different states. There are hundreds of regional dialects.

English is widely spoken throughout the subcontinent. Urdu is the national language of Pakistan, and Punjabi is widely spoken there too. In Bangladesh, 95 per cent of people speak Bengali, having once formed part of the Indian state of Bengal. Sinhala and Tamil are the national languages of Sri Lanka, reflecting the large number of Tamils living on the island. (Tamil is also the language of Tamil Nadu, the southernmost state of India.) Nepali is the national language of Nepal. It is also spoken by about one-quarter of the population of Bhutan, who are settlers from Nepal. Bhutan's official national language is called Dzongkha. It is written in Tibetan script.

The Sherpa people of Nepal respect the mountains as the homes of the gods. The Sherpas themselves are respected as excellent climbers, who are able to carry heavy loads even at high altitudes.

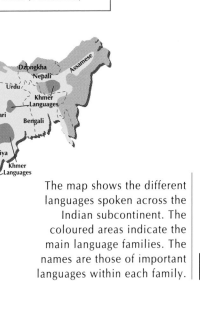

The map shows the different languages spoken across the Indian subcontinent. The coloured areas indicate the main language families. The names are those of important languages within each family.

| Indic | } Indo-European |
| Iranic | } languages |
| Dravidian languages |
| Sino-Tibetan languages |
| Austroasiatic languages |
| Other (Burushaski) |

11

Although the Indian subcontinent is now made up of several independent countries, during the nineteenth and early twentieth centuries most of the region was part of the British Empire. In 1612, the British East India Company set up its first trading post in India at Surat on the coast of Gujarat. By 1690, it also had trading posts in Madras, Bombay and Calcutta, around which the present cities grew up.

At first British interest in the subcontinent was concerned only with trade. By the mid-nineteenth century, however, the British had political control of most of India. (At that time, India included modern-day Pakistan and Bangladesh.) In 1858, the British crown took over control of India from the East India Company and, in 1877, Queen Victoria became Empress of India. Until 1947, India remained part of the British Empire.

The map shows the extent of British India before 1947, and the boundaries created by the division of India in 1947. In 1971, India declared war on Pakistan in support of East Pakistan's claim to be an independent country. East and West Pakistan had been separated by some 1,600 kilometres of Indian territory.

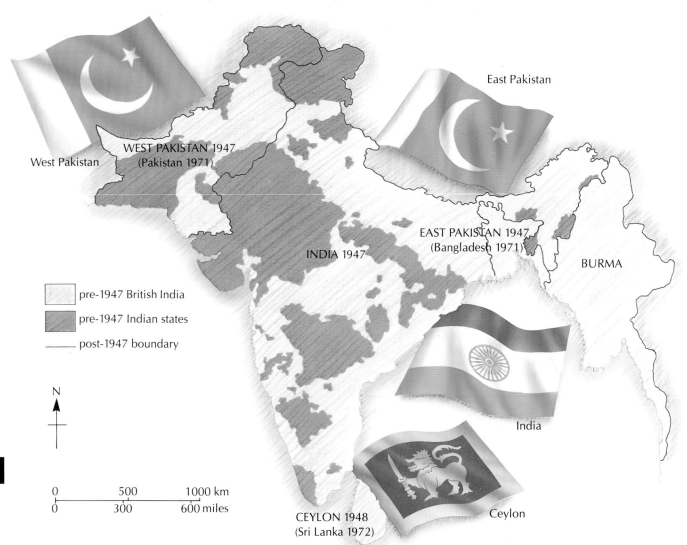

East Pakistan

West Pakistan

WEST PAKISTAN 1947
(Pakistan 1971)

West Pakistan

INDIA 1947

EAST PAKISTAN 1947
(Bangladesh 1971)

BURMA

pre-1947 British India

pre-1947 Indian states

post-1947 boundary

N

India

0   500   1000 km
0   300   600 miles

CEYLON 1948
(Sri Lanka 1972)

Ceylon

Dividing India

In 1947, India gained its independence from Britain. However, the country was split into mainly Hindu India and mainly Muslim Pakistan. But it could not be divided neatly into two. The majority of India's Muslims lived in the western state of Punjab and the eastern state of Bengal, on opposite sides of the country. The new boundaries were drawn through these two states to create West Pakistan and East Pakistan.

The result of the division, or partition, of India was chaos. The man-made boundaries dividing India and Pakistan left millions of people displaced and homeless. For months afterwards, refugees fled backwards and forwards across the new borders, in fear of their lives if they stayed behind. Around 10 million people moved from India to Pakistan and from Pakistan to India. Many were massacred while fleeing from one country to the other. In 1971, East Pakistan became the independent country of Bangladesh.

Muslim refugees in 1947 crowd onto a train bound for Pakistan. They are fleeing from the New Delhi area of India.

Troublespots

Religious differences are the main reasons for the remaining troublespots in the subcontinent. India and Pakistan are still in dispute over the northern state of Kashmir. At the time of India's independence, Kashmir had a mainly Muslim population. However, the state was ruled by a Hindu maharaja who chose to belong to India. Following recent outbreaks of violence, the Indian Army has sent thousands of troops to the region.

Other troublespots include the Indian state of Punjab where many Sikhs are demanding their own state, to be called Khalistan. In Sri Lanka, a Tamil terrorist group, called the Tamil Tigers, has been responsible for violence and bloodshed, including the assassination of the country's president, Ranasinghe Premadasa, in May 1993.

The Sikh Golden Temple in Amritsar in the Indian state of Punjab. Following the partition of India in 1947, Punjab's two major cities, Lahore and Amritsar, were separated from each other. Lahore became part of West Pakistan while Amritsar remained in India.

Regions and religions

The most important factor determining how people on the Indian subcontinent live, where they live and even what they eat, is religion. India was partitioned along religious lines; current troublespots across the subcontinent are largely the result of religious differences. Yet the vast majority of people live together peacefully, whatever their religion.

Followers of seven of the world's major religions live in the Indian subcontinent – Hindus, Muslims, Buddhists, Christians, Sikhs, Jains and Parsis. About 80 per cent of Indians are Hindus. The state religion of Pakistan and Bangladesh, and the very reason for the creation of these countries, is Islam.

The religions of the Indian subcontinent have also played an important part further afield. Many Hindus, Sikhs and Muslims have emigrated from South Asia, taking their religious beliefs and customs with them. In many Western cities, Muslim mosques, Hindu temples and Sikh *gurdwaras* are now built alongside Christian churches and Jewish synagogues.

N

	Hinduism
	Islam
	Buddhism
	Sikhism
	Christianity
	Jainism
	Tribal religions

Amritsar
Indus   Haridwar
        Ayodhya   Himalayas
Mathura   Lumbini
Yamuna   Sarnath
Allahabad   Ganges
Varanasi   Bodh Gaya
Ujjain   Narmada
Dwarka
Godavari
Krishna
Kanchipuram

Sacred place
Sacred river
Sacred mountains

The pie charts show the breakdown of the various religions in four of the subcontinent's countries. Hinduism is the region's dominant religion. (See map, above right, for the colour key to the religions.)

The map shows the distribution of the principal religions of the subcontinent, together with some of the most sacred sites.

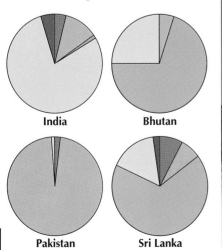

India

Bhutan

Pakistan

Sri Lanka

A Buddhist temple and statue of the Buddha, Sri Lanka. Buddhism was founded in India in about 500 BC. It is now the major religion of Bhutan and Sri Lanka.

Sacred places

Many places in the subcontinent, including geographical features such as mountains and rivers, are considered sacred. Millions of pilgrims visit these places each year. Hindus believe that the Himalayas are the home of one of their most important gods, Shiva. At the time of the full moon in July–August, thousands of people make the *yatra* (pilgrimage) to the Sri Amarnath Cave in the foothills of the Himalayas in Kashmir. Here they worship at a natural ice shrine dedicated to Shiva.

The city of Allahabad lies in northern India at the meeting place of the Ganges and Yamuna rivers. The place where the rivers meet is believed to be particularly good for washing away sins. Every 12 years a special bathing festival, called the Kumbh Mela, is held here. A huge campsite is set up for the millions of pilgrims who attend. A smaller festival is held each year.

These Muslims are praying at the Badshahi Mosque in Lahore, Pakistan. Each year Muslim pilgrims leave the subcontinent for their most important pilgrimage – the Haj – to Mecca in Saudi Arabia. Every Muslim who can is supposed to make the journey at least once in his or her lifetime. Mecca is the birthplace of the prophet Muhammad, the founder of Islam.

Varanasi (left) in northern India is the holiest city of the Hindus. It lies on the banks of the River Ganges. For Hindus, the Ganges is a sacred river. Bathing in its water is believed to wash away a person's sins. Pilgrims bathe from a series of steps, called *ghats*, leading down into the river.

15

Rural life

About four-fifths of the total population of the Indian subcontinent live in villages dotted about the countryside. The majority make their living by farming the land. There are some 580,000 villages in India alone. Some are more like small towns; others are tiny.

This Hindu family in Bangladesh have made their house from bamboo, with a roof of corrugated iron.

Village life

Villages houses are made from local materials, such as mud bricks, covered with mud and cow dung. Cow dung is also dried and used as fuel for the cooking fires. In remote regions, such as the mountains, many villages do not have facilities such as electricity or running water. Many villagers are very poor. The average farmer has only a tiny plot of land to cultivate. This has to provide food to support his family and to sell at market. Many farmers do not own their land. They have to rent it from landlords who may take a proportion of what they grow instead of money. Many villagers are treated unfairly by landlords. Some work as daily labourers on other people's land. But such work is scarce once the harvest is over.

Rural mosque in Sunamganj, Bangladesh. Many villages have temples or mosques, together with small roadside or household shrines.

Life in villages throughout much of the subcontinent is largely traditional. In many places, it has not changed much for hundreds of years. Villages are still very lively places. There are fairs and festivities to celebrate events in the farming year, such as ploughing and harvesting, and on special occasions such as weddings. Even those people who leave their villages, to look for work in the big cities, maintain strong links with their homes. They regularly send money home and return whenever they can. They also tend to marry people from their own village or district.

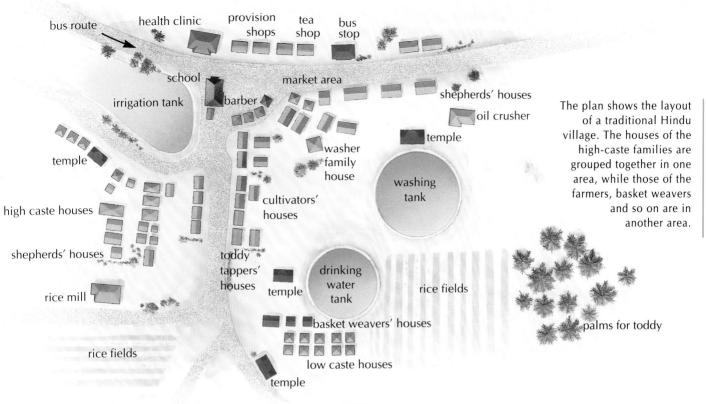

bus route

health clinic

provision shops

tea shop

bus stop

school

market area

shepherds' houses

oil crusher

barber

irrigation tank

temple

temple

washer family house

washing tank

high caste houses

cultivators' houses

shepherds' houses

toddy tappers' houses

drinking water tank

temple

rice fields

rice mill

temple

basket weavers' houses

palms for toddy

rice fields

low caste houses

temple

The plan shows the layout of a traditional Hindu village. The houses of the high-caste families are grouped together in one area, while those of the farmers, basket weavers and so on are in another area.

The well is one of the focal points of the village. It is the women's job to collect water each day.

Family life

All over the subcontinent, family life is extremely important. Many people live in extended families, that is children, parents, grandparents, aunts, uncles and cousins all live together under one roof. From an early age, children help their parents in the fields and with household tasks such as cooking and fetching water from the village well. Some children may attend the village school, which is often held outdoors. Many village families cannot afford to let their children go to school for long, however. They need their help in earning a living

These children are being taught by a village elder in an informal outdoor school.

Farming for food

In every country of the Indian subcontinent, except Sri Lanka, at least half of the workforce is involved in farming. In Nepal and Bhutan, this figure rises to more than 90 per cent. Farms are mostly small and traditional. Most are used for subsistence farming, which means farming for food. More than 50 per cent of India's land area is farmed, and in Bangladesh 65 per cent of the land is cultivated.

Agriculture relies heavily on the monsoon rains, and the types of crop grown reflect the climate. Rice is one of the main crops grown and eaten on the subcontinent. It thrives in the wet conditions. In a drier country like Pakistan, however, where rainfall is low and unreliable, irrigation is essential. Other major food crops include wheat, maize, potatoes, sugar cane, spices, fruit and pulses (lentils, chickpeas and so on).

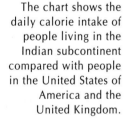

Terraced fields like these ones in Nepal are cut into the mountainsides. By doing this, it is possible for farmers to grow rice on steep, inaccessible land.

Food for thought

The type of food which the people eat depends on where they live and what religion they follow. Along the coasts, people eat fish. Meals are accompanied by rice, if you live in the rice-growing areas of southern India, or bread, if you live in the wheat-growing north.

The chart shows the daily calorie intake of people living in the Indian subcontinent compared with people in the United States of America and the United Kingdom.

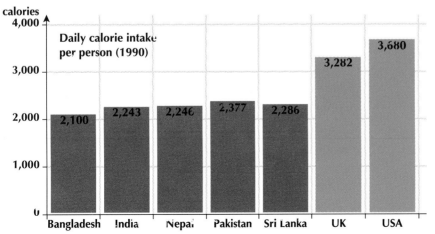

calories

Daily calorie intake per person (1990)

Bangladesh	India	Nepal	Pakistan	Sri Lanka	UK	USA
2,100	2,243	2,246	2,377	2,286	3,282	3,680

Many Hindus are vegetarians, and most never eat beef. Hindus consider cows to be sacred animals. Muslims do not eat pork, which they consider to be unclean. The majority of people cannot afford a particularly healthy diet. In Bangladesh and Bhutan, not enough food is produced to feed everyone properly. In Bhutan, the problem is made worse by the hilly, inhospitable land which makes farming difficult and time consuming.

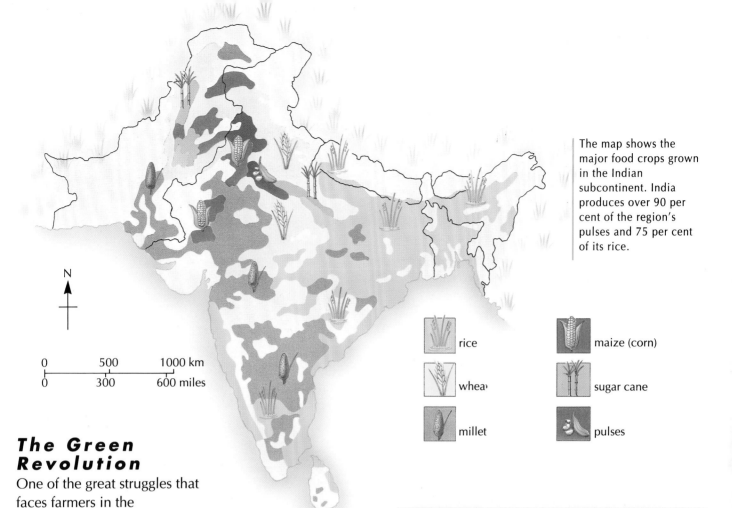

The map shows the major food crops grown in the Indian subcontinent. India produces over 90 per cent of the region's pulses and 75 per cent of its rice.

0 500 1000 km
0 300 600 miles

- rice
- wheat
- millet
- maize (corn)
- sugar cane
- pulses

The Green Revolution

One of the great struggles that faces farmers in the subcontinent is to produce enough food for the growing populations of their countries. In the past, food production could not keep up with demand, and countries had to import expensive food supplies. However, one of India's major successes since Independence in 1947 has been its progress towards self-sufficiency in food. The Indian government also has large quantities of grain in emergency storage, to prevent famine if harvests fail. The reason for this success was the so-called Green Revolution of the late 1960s. Higher-yielding types of wheat and rice seed were developed, and the use of fertilisers was increased.

These farmers are growing wheat in the Punjab northern Pakistan Across the border in India, the state of Punjab is known as the 'granary of India' because of the huge amounts of wheat grown there.

Surplus fruit and vegetables are sold at daily or weekly markets like this one at Matara on Sri Lanka's south coast.

Farming for export

Many of the crops that are grown for use within the Indian subcontinent are also grown as crops for export (cash crops). The major export crops are cotton, jute, tea and cardamom and other spices. It was India's spices, as well as its brightly coloured silks and satins, which attracted European traders to South Asia in the sixteenth and seventeenth centuries. The export crops are exported to other countries within the subcontinent and further afield.

India

India's main cash crops are cotton, tea, rice, cashew nuts and spices. It also produces large quantities of groundnuts, sugar cane, coffee, leather and some jute for export. India's main export partners are the former USSR, the USA, Japan, the United Kingdom and Germany.

The map shows where the subcontinent's major export crops are grown, as well as the principal export crops of the four larger countries. The figures are percentages of each country's total exports.

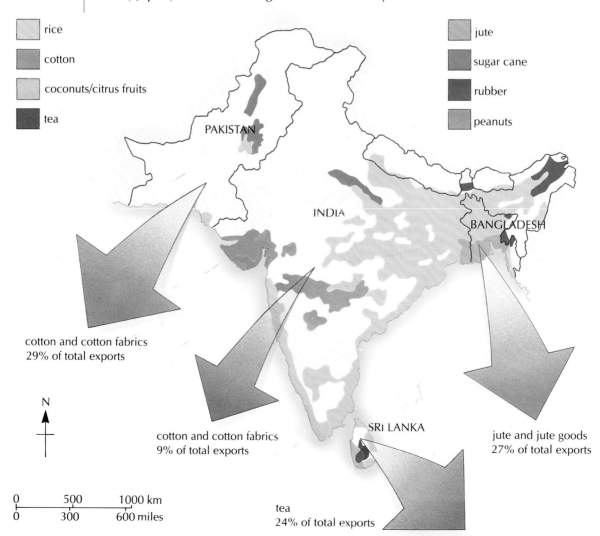

- rice
- cotton
- coconuts/citrus fruits
- tea

- jute
- sugar cane
- rubber
- peanuts

PAKISTAN

INDIA

BANGLADESH

SRI LANKA

cotton and cotton fabrics
29% of total exports

cotton and cotton fabrics
9% of total exports

jute and jute goods
27% of total exports

tea
24% of total exports

N

0	500	1000 km
0	300	600 miles

Pakistan

Cotton and rice are Pakistan's major cash crops. It also exports fish and leather. Cotton is exported in its raw state, as cotton thread, as fabric or as ready-made clothes. Pakistan mainly exports these items to the USA, Japan, Germany, the United Kingdom and Saudi Arabia.

Bangladesh

Bangladesh's most important export crop is jute. This is a crop which flourishes in the damp climate and soils of the delta lands. When Bengal was partitioned in 1947, the jute mills and port remained on the Indian side of the dividing line, while East Pakistan was left with plenty of jute but not a single mill for processing it. Bangladesh exports to the USA, Italy, the United Kingdom, Singapore and Germany. It also exports fish and leather.

Tea pickers on a plantation near Nuwara Eliya in Sri Lanka. The areas of Assam and Darjeeling in India are also famous for their tea plantations.

Sri Lanka

In 1990, Sri Lanka overtook India as the world's top exporter of tea. It also exports rubber, coconuts and precious stones such as emeralds and rubies to the USA, Germany, the United Kingdom, Japan and Iran. Many of Sri Lanka's cash crops are grown on huge plantations, rather than on smallholdings.

These workers in Bangladesh are stripping bark from the stems of jute plants. The stringy fibres of the jute plant can be used to make rope and rough cloth for sacking.

Nepal

Jute, leather and pulses are Nepal's main export crops. They are exported to India, Germany, the USA, Belgium and the United Kingdom.

Bhutan

Bhutan is one of the world's biggest producers of cardamom spice. Timber and fruit, especially oranges, are other important cash crops. Over 90 per cent of Bhutan's export crops are sent to India.

Cotton is the most important fibre grown for export. Like rice, it is a crop which needs to be kept well watered. This cotton has been harvested in the Sind Province of Pakistan. India is now the world's fourth largest producer of cotton, after the USA, China and the former USSR.

Handicrafts and heavy industry

Since Indian Independence in 1947, industry throughout the subcontinent has expanded quickly. India, for example, now ranks among the world's top 12 industrialised nations in terms of the quantity of goods it produces. However, it is not just major industries such as engineering or iron and steel production which are important. Small-scale industry, including family-run handicraft businesses, are responsible for about half of India's industrial output. These so-called 'cottage' industries are vital to the economies of all the countries in the subcontinent.

A Nepalese woman weaves cloth outside her home. Less than five per cent of Nepal's population works in industry.

Handicrafts

Textiles and handicrafts from the Indian subcontinent are sold all over the world. These are largely produced by traditional village businesses in which skills are handed down from one generation to the next. Traditional textile designs include embroidery, block printing, mirror work and tie-dye. Handicrafts include carpets and papier-mâché goods from Kashmir; basketwork from Nepal; statues carved from fragrant sandalwood or cast in bronze, and exquisite jewellery made from locally mined gold and precious stones.

Natural resources

Industry relies on natural resources. The subcontinent has a wide range of mineral resources but they are not shared out evenly between the different countries. India has huge stocks of iron ore and coal which have allowed it to develop a thriving steel industry. About 12 million tonnes of steel are produced each year. It is used to make cars, bicycles, motorbikes and so on. One of India's most heavily industrialised areas lies around the city of Jamshedpur in the Damodar Valley near Calcutta. Because of its position near major iron ore and coal deposits, it has become a centre of iron and steel production.

Steelworks at Jamshedpur, India.

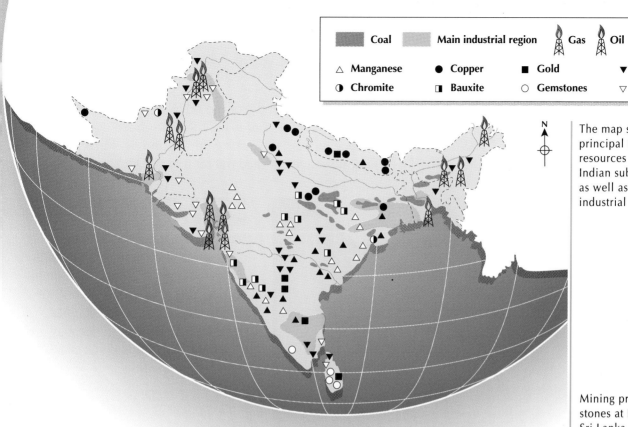

Coal	Main industrial region	Gas	Oil	▲ Iron ore
△ Manganese	● Copper	■ Gold		▼ Limestone
◑ Chromite	▣ Bauxite	○ Gemstones		▽ Salt

The map shows the principal mineral resources of the Indian subcontinent, as well as its main industrial regions.

Mining precious stones at Ratnapura, Sri Lanka.

Pakistan's main mineral export is oil. Chromite, limestone and rock salt are also mined. Large quantities of gemstones are mined in Sri Lanka and exported abroad. Bangladesh has very few natural resources, apart from natural gas. The textile industry is a major source of its foreign earnings. It has to import fuel, metals and machinery. Talc is Bhutan's main export mineral but it has reserves of other minerals, such as limestone and dolomite, which have not yet been fully exploited.

Water power

The mighty rivers of the subcontinent are able to provide certain countries with cheap and plentiful hydro-electricity. Hydro-electric power provided by fast-flowing mountain rivers is the principal energy esource of Sri Lanka, Nepal and Bhutan. In 1986, the Chukha hydro-electric project was launched in Bhutan to provide inexpensive electricity for use at home and for export. Pakistan has also been able to produce valuable hydro-electricity from its three major rivers – the Indus, the Jhelum and the Kabul.

This dam at Tarbela near Rawalpindi, Pakistan, is the world's largest earth-filled dam. About half of Pakistan's electricity comes from hydro-electric power stations.

Help for the environment

Many of the illnesses suffered by people in the subcontinent are carried by water. These water-borne illnesses include typhoid, hepatitis, cholera, diarrhoea and dysentery. They are often fatal.

As the subcontinent has developed its industry and agriculture, serious damage has been done to its environment. Smoke, fumes and discharge from factories have polluted the air and water.

Dirty air and water

Many of the subcontinent's biggest cities suffer from serious air pollution, caused mainly by smoke and fumes from factories and cars. Levels of poisonous gases such as sulphur dioxide in Calcutta and Bombay are above the safe limits set by the World Health Organisation.

Very few towns throughout the subcontinent have an adequate sewage system. Human waste (together with animal waste and factory run-off) is often dumped straight into the nearest river. As a result, many of the region's most important rivers, such as the Ganges, the Indus and the Narmada, are severely polluted. About one-quarter of the total length of the River Ganges is so polluted that it has become a health hazard. The Central Ganges Authority was set up in 1985 to clean up the river and organise the building of new sewage treatment plants. Its task is an enormous one.

Clearing the forests

Soil erosion and deforestation are becoming widespread. Forests are being destroyed at an alarming rate for fuelwood, to clear space for mines and for the building of huge hydro-electric and irrigation dams. One of the largest schemes is the vast irrigation and dam project along India's Narmada River.

In India, local conservation groups are now working with the government to protect the environment. A massive reafforestation programme has been set up to plant millions of new trees.

On 2 December 1984, poisonous gas leaked from the Union Carbide pesticide factory in Bhopal, India. It killed 2,000 people and injured hundreds of thousands more in the nearby shanty towns. Many of these people died later.

The map shows the location of the subcontinent's most polluted rivers and of its national parks.

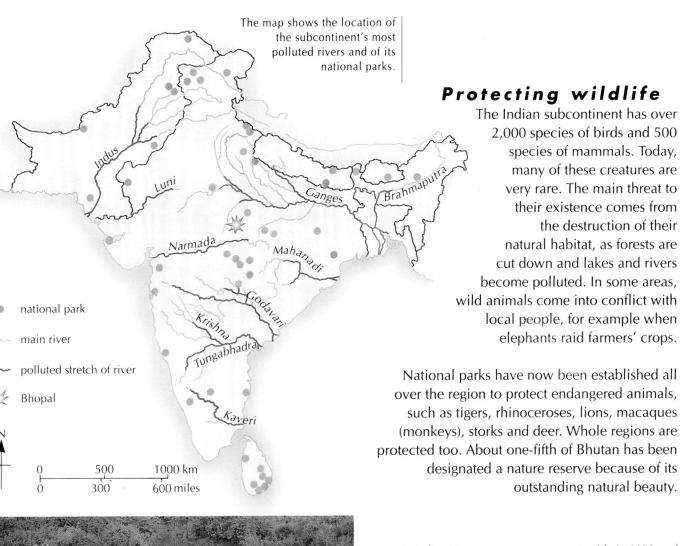

● national park

~ main river

~ polluted stretch of river

✳ Bhopal

N

| 0 | 500 | 1000 km |
| 0 | 300 | 600 miles |

Protecting wildlife

The Indian subcontinent has over 2,000 species of birds and 500 species of mammals. Today, many of these creatures are very rare. The main threat to their existence comes from the destruction of their natural habitat, as forests are cut down and lakes and rivers become polluted. In some areas, wild animals come into conflict with local people, for example when elephants raid farmers' crops.

National parks have now been established all over the region to protect endangered animals, such as tigers, rhinoceroses, lions, macaques (monkeys), storks and deer. Whole regions are protected too. About one-fifth of Bhutan has been designated a nature reserve because of its outstanding natural beauty.

In India, 15 nature reserves were set aside in 1973 as part of Project Tiger. The project aimed to save the Indian tiger from extinction. Since 1900, tiger numbers had dropped from thousands to hundreds. They have now begun to rise again, and there are between 3,000 and 4,000 tigers.

The Sundarbans is the world's largest mangrove forest. It stretches over thousands of square kilometres across the Ganges Delta in India and Bangladesh. The area is an important spawning ground for fish and shellfish, which provide local people with work. The mangrove trees also help to protect the coast from damage by cyclones.

Cities and crowds

The majority of people in the subcontinent live in the countryside, although the urban population is growing fast throughout the region. This is mainly due to the large numbers of people who come to the cities from the countryside in search of work. Bombay is the biggest city on the subcontinent, with some 12.5 million inhabitants in the city and surrounding area. Three of the biggest cities in India – Calcutta, Bombay and Madras – grew up around important ports and trading posts established by the East India Company.

About one-fifth of city dwellers live in slums or shanty towns, or even on the streets, like this family.

City life

The cities of the subcontinent are mostly crowded, bustling places. Overloaded buses share the packed streets with rickshaws, hooting cars, taxis, people and even sacred cows. People from the countryside may get jobs as rickshaw or taxi drivers, in hotels or as servants to wealthy families. Many live in crowded shanty towns or slums, often with no access to clean water or to sewage facilities. Outbreaks of diseases such as typhoid and dysentery are common in these places. In some cities, the authorities have now accepted that the shanty towns are here to stay, and are trying to improve conditions for the people living in them.

A view of Bombay shows the contrast between modern high-rise buildings and the shanty towns of the poor.

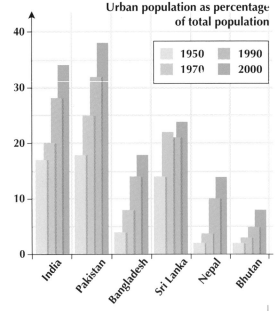

Urban population as percentage of total population

Legend: 1950, 1970, 1990, 2000

(Countries: India, Pakistan, Bangladesh, Sri Lanka, Nepal, Bhutan)

The chart shows how much the urban population has increased over the past 40 years, and its projected increase into the year 2000.

The transport system

The cities of the Indian subcontinent are linked by a vast transport network. Travel is possible by air, rail, bus, car, bullock cart and, if you live in the desert, by camel. India has the fourth largest railway system in the world. The British had the first tracks laid in the mid-nineteenth century, to make it easier to travel around India and to govern the country. The railways also helped to unite the country by linking remote villages. Today there are more than 60,000 kilometres of track, and the railways carry about 3.5 billion passengers each year.

Travel abroad

In the nineteenth and early twentieth centuries, many people from India (which then included Pakistan and Bangladesh) travelled abroad to work on European sugar, coffee, tea and rubber plantations. They were badly paid, and often badly treated. Since Independence in 1947, hundreds of thousands of Indians have left the subcontinent to live and work abroad. Many have gone to the United Kingdom; others have settled in the West Indies and the Middle East.

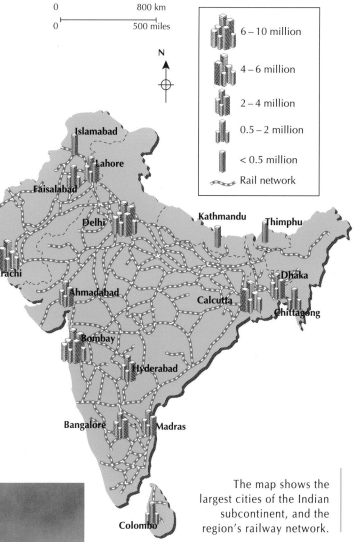

The map shows the largest cities of the Indian subcontinent, and the region's railway network.

A crowded passenger train in Tamil Nadu, southern India.

27

*L*ooking forwards

The countries of the Indian subcontinent face many problems as they look towards the future. They must try to control the increase in their populations. Also, they must work towards improving health and welfare services. They must also try to resolve the conflicts between members of different religious and ethnic groups. These conflicts threaten the stability of areas of the subcontinent. Governments have already begun to tackle some of these problems.

The map shows member countries of the Commonwealth of Nations and of the Non-Aligned Movement.

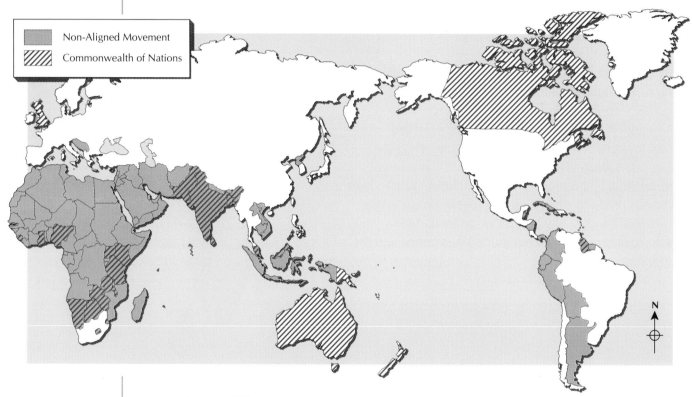

Non-Aligned Movement
Commonwealth of Nations

World affairs

The Indian subcontinent plays an important role in world affairs. India, Pakistan, Bangladesh and Sri Lanka are members of the Commonwealth of Nations. This is an association of most of the former colonies of the British Empire. They are all equal partners, with the British Queen as the nominal head of the Commonwealth. All the countries of the subcontinent belong to the Non-Aligned Movement (NAM). The NAM is not linked politically to either the USA or the former USSR. The countries of the subcontinent also belong to the South Asia Regional Co-operation Organisation (SAARC).

Local people in Jodhpur, India, listen to an election speech. India is the world's most populous democracy.

Facing the future

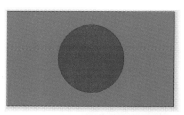

Bangladesh
The People's Republic of Bangladesh is one of the poorest countries in the world. Its problems in the future include trying to grow enough food to feed its people. In addition, Bangladesh regularly has to cope with major natural disasters, such as cyclones and serious floods.

Bhutan
Bhutan has close political links with India. In 1990 there were violent demonstrations against the Bhutanese government by Nepalese settlers living in the south of the country. The unrest continues.

India
The future problems of this huge democracy include continuing population growth and repeated outbreaks of violence between Hindus and Muslims. However, India has made great strides in the fields of science and technology, including space and agricultural research.

Nepal
Following protests for a more democratic government, Nepal has been ruled by an elected government since the early 1990s. There is still political unrest in the country, and many people are desperately poor. Nepal has renewed its trade links with India, hoping to improve its economic situation. Recently, it has become a popular tourist destination for trekkers and climbers.

Pakistan
The Islamic Republic of Pakistan has had a turbulent political history since independence in 1947. Political unrest continues in Pakistan, together with religious and territorial conflicts with India. Pakistan has an important role to play as one of the leading nations of the Indian subcontinent.

Sri Lanka
Sri Lanka's most urgent problem is to resolve the conflict between the government and a terrorist group called the Tamil Tigers. The group claims to represent the rights of the minority Tamil population in Sri Lanka. The Tamils originally came from the southern Indian state of Tamil Nadu.

Databank

Physical geography

- The Himalayas are between 150 and 400 kilometres wide, and 2,500 kilometres long from north-west to south-east. Only 14 of the world's mountains are over 8,000 metres high, and all 14 are in the Himalayas.
- The world's land areas were once all joined together in a giant supercontinent called Pangaea. About 200 million years ago Pangaea began to split in two. By 80 million years ago India had broken away from Australia and Antarctica. It then began to move northwards.
- The amount of rainfall divides Sri Lanka into two distinct regions: the Wet Zone in the south-west, and the Dry Zone which covers the rest of the island.
- People in Tamil Nadu, the most southerly state in India, are more than 2,000 kilometres away from the Indian capital, New Delhi. That is about the same distance as between London and the city of Athens in Greece.

People

- India was the first country in the world to have a national family planning programme. It was set up in 1952.
- About 40 per cent of people in the Indian subcontinent are below the age of 15.
- More children work in India than in any other country. They are mostly children from poor rural areas whose parents need them to help in the fields as well as in the home.
- The population of the Indian subcontinent between 1950 and 1990, and the estimated population figures for the year 2000:

| country | population (millions) | | | | | |
	1950	1960	1970	1980	1990	2000 (est.)
India	350.4	431 5	551.3	689.06	827.1	1,041.5
Pakistan	40.0	50.1	63.7	87.1	112.1	162.4
Bangladesh*	42.3	51.6	66.7	88.2	115.6	150.6
Sri Lanka	7.7	9.9	12.5	14.8	17.2	19.4
Nepal	8.2	9.4	11.5	14.9	19.1	24.1
Bhutan	0.7	0.9	1.0	1.3	1.5	1.9
* East Pakistan until 1971.						

Religion

- When a Muslim baby is born, the call to prayer is whispered into the baby's right ear and the start of prayer into the left ear. The baby is named seven days later, in a ceremony called the *aqiqah*.

- According to tradition, Sikh men must wear or carry five signs of their religion. These are known as the five 'Ks'. They are *kes* (uncut hair and beard), *kangha* (a comb), *kirpan* (a dagger), *kara* (a steel bangle) and *kachh* (shorts).
- All Sikh men have the title 'Singh' (Lion), and all Sikh women the title 'Kaur' (Princess).

Language and education

- Hindi is the official language of India. It is the fourth most widely spoken language in the world.
- India has the third highest number of students in higher education in the world, after the USA and the former USSR.
- Many students study religious texts and subjects such as language, philosophy, mathematics, logic and astronomy.
- In Bhutan, tuition, textbooks, uniform, and board and lodging if necessary, are provided free of charge in primary schools. This is to encourage pupils to attend school.

Environment

- One of the best-known environmental groups in India is the Chipko Andolan (the Chipko Movement). Its aim is to save India's forests from destruction. The movement began in the early 1970s when a group of village women hugged nearby trees to stop them from being cut down.
- India's forests are being destroyed at a rate of 147,000 hectares each year.
- It is estimated that about 73 million working days are lost in India each year through water-borne illnesses such as cholera and typhoid.

Politics

- India has an electorate of more than 450 million people (1988).
- The main political parties in India are: the Indian National Congress, the Janata Dal (a coalition party), the Communist Party and the BJP (Bharatiya Janata party).
- The Indian constitution allows seats in the parliament building to be reserved for the scheduled castes (who used to be known as the 'untouchables') and for the tribes.
- Bhutan's head of state is the king, who is called the Druk Gyalpo. In the villages, decisions affecting the local population are taken by the village headmen.
- Three countries of the Indian subcontinent have had women prime ministers: India (Indira Gandhi), Pakistan (Benazir Bhutto) and Sri Lanka (Sirimavo Bandaranaike).

Glossary

batik
A method of making patterns on cloth by using wax.

calorie
A measurement that tells how much energy is contained in different foods.

cardamom
A type of spice used in many of the subcontinent's dishes.

cash crop
A crop that is grown for sale abroad. In the Indian subcontinent, important cash crops are cotton and tea.

cyclone
A powerful tropical storm that brings heavy rain and strong winds. Cyclones can cause terrible destruction and loss of life. They are a type of hurricane.

delta
An area of low-lying land that forms where a river flows into the sea.

family planning
Different methods that are used to reduce the number of babies that are born each year.

fold mountain
A mountain which was formed when two pieces of the Earth's crust crashed into each other. The crust between them was pushed up into gigantic folds.

hydro-electric power
Electricity which is made from the energy produced by fast-moving water.

irrigation
Taking water from rivers and dams to farmland where it is needed. The water is moved from place to place along canals, channels and pipes.

life expectancy
The average number of years that a person can expect to live.

monsoon
A wind which blows across Asia and changes direction according to the time of the year. It can bring heavy rains.

natural resource
Any material which is found naturally in a country, such as coal, water, forests, fish, etc.

partition
Another word for division.

plate
One of the large pieces of the outer layer, or crust, that surrounds the Earth.

refugee
A person who is forced to leave or flee their country because of war, famine or unrest.

rickshaw
A two-wheeled vehicle which is used for transporting people and goods.

self-sufficiency
Self-sufficiency in food means that a country can grow and produce enough food to feed its people, without having to import food from other countries.

silt
Rich fertile soil that is deposited by a river.

subcontinent
A huge area of land which is already part of a continent. A subcontinent can be as big as an actual continent.

tie-dye
A way of creating a pattern on cloth by tying the cloth with string and then dyeing it.

Index